Chips

Top Chips

Crispy, fat-free and easy-to-make chips may once have sounded too good to be true—but not anymore, thanks to Mastrad's TopChips!

A 3.5-oz serving of potato chips made with Mastrad's TopChips contains 320 kcal*, 0 grams** fat and only 30 mg** sodium (salt).

Not only are fruit and vegetable chips made with the TopChips light, airy and healthful: they are also simply delicious. Easy to make, these chips will play a starring role at your picnics and will be the perfect side dish to your main courses and before-dinner drinks.

Discover American chef Camille Renk's and French chef Jean-Claude Fascina's original recipes using the TopChips!

* compared to more than 500 kcal in store-bought chips, ** compared to more than 30 grams in store-bought chips, *** compared to more than 500 grams in store-bought chips

Chips, anyone?
All kinds of chips served in all kinds of ways!

With TopChips, you can have your chips and eat them too! Whether going on a picnic or serving a meal in your home or backyard, you can prepare whatever you're in the mood for by whipping up a batch of your very own fruit or vegetable chips ahead of time.

Guests will love biting into a crispy potato or sweet potato chip along with raw veggies and fresh herbs (basil) or cooked and chilled vegetables (ratatouille, stewed tomatoes, zucchini, or eggplant).

Mango chips are delicious served with shrimp or smoked fish (salmon, trout, haddock).

Potato, sweet potato, apple, and pear chips add a welcome crunch to cold cuts and poultry.

Apple and pear chips are also the perfect accompaniment to cheese (hard cheeses like Gruyère or Comté, and medium/soft cheeses like Morbier, blue cheese and sheep's milk cheese) which you can cut into shavings or cubes beforehand.

Sweet potato and mango chips add a delightful crunch to tabbouleh.

Apple and pear chips bring a touch of sweetness to pasta or grain salads.

Note!: Recommended ingredients for use on TopChips are potatoes, sweet potatoes, carrots, mangoes, apples and pears. Always monitor cooking.

You should not use any kind of beets or basil on TopChips.

Instructions for using TopChips

Designed for use in a microwave oven, Mastrad's TopChips allows you to make chips in just a few minutes without using any fat at all.

Made from food grade silicone, the TopChips is flexible, non-stick and unbreakable. TopChips can withstand exposure to temperatures up to 420°F and is easy to clean and dishwasher safe.
You can stack up to three TopChips at a time.

Use & care

Only use TopChips in a microwave. If you have a combined microwave/grill oven, only use the microwave function. If your oven is equipped with a rotating tray, make sure that it can move freely.

Place the TopChips tray (covered in potato, fruit or vegetables) in the microwave and begin cooking.

The cooking times for different kinds of chips are listed on pages 12-13.

When using additional TopChips trays, stack them on top of one another (limit of three at a time) and increase the cooking time by one minute per tray.

The listed cooking times are recommendations only. Many factors can considerably alter the ideal cooking time: your microwave oven's general condition (how old and clean it is) and power; the origin, ripeness, and water content of the food you are using; and the thickness and consistency of your slices.
If necessary, adjust the cooking time by thirty-second intervals. To avoid overcooking, which can cause unnecessary wear to your TopChips, always keep an eye on your chips.

Peel, wash and dry your fruit and/or vegetable using a paper towel.

For best results, cut the fruit and/or vegetable into thin, even slices with the mandolin included in the TopChips kit. Otherwise, cut uniform, 1-mm-thick slices with a knife.

Arrange the thinly cut slices on the TopChips, making sure that they do not overlap.

the basics

Place the TopChips in the microwave and begin cooking. Set the cooking time according to the recommended times listed in the table p.12-13.

Once cooked, let the chips cool for 30 seconds on the TopChips before removing them with care.

Season and enjoy!

	POTATO	SWEET POTATO	CARROT
1000 W	3 min.	3 min.	3 min.
850 W	4 min.	3 ½ min.	5 min.
750 W	5 min.	5 min.	5 ½ min.
TopChips seasoning	BBQ, salt & vinegar, sour cream & onion, roasted garlic	BBQ, salt & vinegar, sour cream & onion, roasted garlic	BBQ, salt & vinegar, sour cream & onion, roasted garlic, apple pie
Seasoning suggestions	Prior to cooking, sprinkle with: spices (cinnamon, turmeric, paprika, Espelette pepper, nutmeg, saffron), flavored peppers, flavored salts, dried herbs (aneth, herbes de Provence, chives, thyme, rosemary, sage, oregano, marjoram).	Prior to cooking, sprinkle with: spices (cinnamon, Espelette pepper, cumin, ground ginger, ras el hanout, Caribbean curry powder, curry, nutmeg), flavored peppers, flavored salts, dried herbs (herbes de Provence, sage, tarragon, fennel).	Prior to cooking, sprinkle with: spices (cumin, ground ginger) or dried herbs (mint, fennel).

Recommendations for cooking

Follow the chat above the best results when using the TopChips™. The chart contains recommendations only. Factor such as a particular microwave, its age, and thickness of food slices, can significantly impact recommended cooking time.

	MANGO	APPLE	PEAR	HERBS: dill, coriander, chives, tarragon, chervil*	ONION	GARLIC	GINGER
1000 W	4 min.	3 ½ min.	3 min.	1 min.	3 min.	2 ½ min.	3 min.
850 W	4 ½ min.	4 ½ min.	3 ½ min.	1 min.	4 min.	3 ½ min.	4 min.
750 W	10 min.	5 ½ min.	4 min.	1 ½ min.	4 ½ min.	4 ½ min	5 min
TopChips seasoning	Apple pie, roasted garlic, sour cream & onion	Apple pie, roasted garlic, sour cream & onion	Apple pie, roasted garlic, sour cream & onion				
Seasoning suggestions		Prior to cooking, sprinkle with: spices (cinnamon, gingerbread spices, allspice), vanilla seeds.	Prior to cooking, sprinkle with: spices (cinnamon), grated tonka bean, ground sugared almonds, powdered tea.				Prior to cooking, sprinkle with: spices (ground ginger, curry).

*Do not use basil on your TopChips

Helpful hints

When cooking potatoes, dry them first using a paper towel before placing them on the the TopChips™.

Thanks to a new range of spices specially created by Mastrad to add even more flavor to your chips, you can now try your hand at original and tasty snacks whenever you like.

Mastrad's spices are made from all-natural ingredients and do not contain any additives or MSGs. They are available in five sweet and savory flavors that you can sprinkle over your fruit or vegetable chips prior to or after cooking.

For a savory snack, add a dusting of Roasted Garlic, BBQ, Salt & Vinegar, or Sour Cream & Onion seasoning to your potato or vegetable chips.

Enhance the flavor of your fruit chips, especially apple and pear, with a sprinkling of the cinnamon-spiced Apple Pie mix.

By mixing a few pinches of certain spices, the sky's the limit when it comes to your chips' flavor. With its endless possibilities, your TopChips is sure to become your cooking partner of choice, as you delight yourself and your guests with your mouthwatering concoctions. Mastrad's special chip spices will transform your chips into gourmet treats that you and your friends and family can enjoy anytime!

So unleash your inner chef and let your imagination run wild!

Roasted Garlic

Apple Pie

Sour Cream
& Onion

BBQ

Salt &
Vinegar

Italian pesto dip with fingerling potato chips

Ingredients

For the dip:

1 small eggplant

2 teaspoons sea salt

¼ cup olive oil

1 red pepper

½ sweet onion

2 Roma tomatoes

½ cup ricotta cheese

½ cup basil leaves

Sea salt and pepper

For the chips:

6 fingerling potatoes

1 Italian Pesto Dip: Cut the eggplant into 1-inch cubes, toss it with the sea salt and let sit for 30 mn. Drain the eggplant, rinse it and set it aside.

2 Chop the onion.
Stem, seed and halve the red pepper. Roast the onion and red pepper in a heavy pan over medium-high heat until they are translucent and slightly caramelized.

3 Add the eggplant and cook until soft (about 8-10 mn). Add the halved tomatoes and cook until soft (about 5 mn).

4 Transfer the vegetable mixture to a food processor and add the ricotta and basil. Pulse until slightly chunky. Season to taste with sea salt and pepper.

5 Fingerling Potato Chips: Cut the potatoes into slices using the food slicer. Arrange the slices on the TopChips and cook in the microwave (refer to the instructions in The Basics).

Tip

Add TopChips Roasted Garlic seasoning to your chips for extra flavor.

Braised artichokes dips with fingerling potato chips

Ingredients

For the dip:

2 tablespoons extra virgin olive oil

4 garlic cloves

Juice of ½ lemon

½ cup white wine

¼ cup chicken broth

6 large artichokes

Sea salt and pepper

½ red jalapeno pepper

2 tsp chopped fresh thyme

For the chips:

6 large fingerling potatoes

1 Artichoke Prep: Cut stem of artichoke flush with bottom.
Peel off and discard outer leaves until you are left with light colored tender leaves.
Use sharp scissors and cut just above the heart. Remove inside purple tipped leaves.
Use a melon baller and scrape out the fuzzy choke.
Trim bottom of heart, removing all tough, fibrous, dark green parts.
Place in bowl of lemon water to prevent heart from turning brown.

2 Heat a non stick pan over medium-high heat. Add oil, artichokes and sauté for 1 mn. Add finely chopped garlic and seeded, eminced jalapeno.
Continue cooking until artichokes are just starting to caramelize.
Deglaze with white wine, then add lemon juice and chicken broth. Bring to a boil, add thyme, then reduce heat until artichokes are tender.
Season with salt and pepper

3 Fingerling potato chip: Slice potato using a food slicer. Place on TopChips. Cook in microwave according to the instructions in The Basics.

White bean and garlic dip with fingerling potato chips

Ingredients

For the dip:

2 cups cooked white beans

5 cloves garlic

3 tablespoon olive oil

2 tablespoons fresh lemon juice

1 sprig fresh rosemary

1 teaspoon Italian parsley

¼ teaspoon dried red chili pepper

Sea salt and freshly ground pepper

For the chips:

6 fingerling potatoes

1 **White Bean and Rosemary Garlic Dip:** Slice off the top third of the garlic head, so that the cloves are exposed. Place the head of unpeeled cloves on a baking sheet lined with wax paper and drizzle with olive oil. Cover with aluminum foil and bake at 175°C / 350°F for 30 mn.

2 Remove the foil and continue baking until the garlic is soft and turns a nice golden color (about 20-25 mn). Cool slightly before removing the garlic cloves from the head.

3 In a food processor, combine the cooked beans, roasted garlic, lemon juice, rosemary, parsley and chili pepper. Pulse until smooth and season to taste with sea salt and freshly ground pepper.

4 **Fingerling Potato Chips:** Cut the potatoes into slices using the food slicer. Arrange the slices on the TopChips and cook in the microwave (refer to the instructions in The Basics).

 Tip
Extra dip can be used on sandwiches, great with grilled vegetable sandwiches.

Herby cheese mousse with apple & pear chips

Ingredients

For the dip:

200 g/ 7 oz cottage cheese

½ bunch fresh coriander

½ bunch chervil

½ bunch flat parsley

1 drizzle olive oil

Salt, ground pepper

For the chips:

1 pear

1 apple

1 Chips: Prepare the pear and apple chips with the Top Chips as indicated in The Basics.

2 Dip: Pour the cottage cheese in a round bottomed bowl. Whisk together with the olive oil, salt and ground pepper.

3 Very finely chop the fresh herbs, add them to the cottage cheese and mix thoroughly. Cover and keep in the fridge until ready to serve.

4 Presentation: Present the sauce and the chips in small bowls and eat straight away!

More dips

Fruit and vegetable chips made with TopChips are perfect for dipping.

A Few More Ideas

Healthful dips made from **plain or Greek-style yogurt, silken tofu, soy cream,** or **coconut milk** will be the ideal match for your light chips. Season these bases to your liking with fresh or dried herbs, spices, pieces of dried fruit and fresh fruit or vegetable coulis.

For example, mix silken tofu with some freshly chopped coriander and fine-brunoise-cut yellow, red and green bell peppers.

For a more exotic dip, try seasoning puréed sweet potatoes with curry and sesame seeds. You can also mix avocado with fresh coriander, lemon juice and a pinch of freshly grated ginger.

dips

A Few More Recipes

Curry Dip:
(Ingredients: 1 egg yolk, 1 tablespoon mustard, salt and freshly ground pepper, grape-seed oil, 1 teaspoon curry paste)

In a bowl, mix the egg yolk with the mustard and season with salt and pepper. Gradually add the oil, whisking until you obtain a mayonnaise-like consistency. Gently incorporate the curry paste, cover and refrigerate.

Coriander Dip:
(Ingredients: 1 cup Greek-style yogurt, 1 teaspoon chopped coriander, 1 pinch Cayenne pepper)

Pour the yogurt into a bowl and whisk in the chopped coriander and Cayenne pepper. Cover and refrigerate.

Soy Sauce Dip:
(Ingredients: 4 tablespoons soy sauce, 1 tablespoon honey, 1 teaspoon freshly grated ginger, 1 tablespoon fresh pineapple, diced, 1 pinch salt)

In a bowl, whisk together the soy sauce and honey. Add the ginger, pineapple and salt. Cover and leave at room temperature.

Hors d'oeuvres

Apple chips and blue cheese sandwiches

Ingredients

For the filling:

8.4 fl oz whipping cream
(minimum fat content: 30%)

3.5 oz soft blue cheese

Salt, freshly ground pepper

Fleur de sel

For the chips:

3 Golden Delicious apples

1 pinch all-spice

1 pinch paprika

1 Chips: Use the TopChips to make
40 apple chips (refer to the instructions in
The Basics).
Sprinkle the apple slices with all-spice and
paprika before cooking.

2 Filling: Pour the whipping cream into
a heavy saucepan and heat over low heat.
Crumble the blue cheese into the cream
and heat until the cheese has melted
completely.
Strain the cheese mixture and chill before
whipping with a whisk or eggbeater.

3 Assembly: To serve place a few dabs of
whipped blue-cheese cream on 20 chips.
Sandwich each chip with an identically
sized chip and garnish each "sandwich"
with a half-chip.
Sprinkle with *fleur de sel* and enjoy
immediately!

Tip

Add TopChips BBQ seasoning to your chips for extra flavor.

Caramelized onions with goat cheese & yukon gold potato chips

Ingredients

For the onions:

1 tablespoon olive oil

1 large sweet onion

sea salt and pepper to taste

½ tablespoon sugar

For the goat cheese:

4 oz goat cheese

1 tablespoons extra-virgin olive oil

sea salt and freshly ground pepper

For the chips:

2 Yukon gold potatoes

Garnish:

4 Black Mission figs

2 tablespoon honey

1 Caramelized Onions:
Heat oil in sauté pan over medium-high heat. Add onions, sprinkle with sugar and season with salt and pepper. Cook stirring occasionally until onions have caramelized, about 10-20 mn.

2 Goat Cheese:
Using your mixer's paddle attachment, beat the goat cheese and 1 tablespoon olive oil. Add a little more oil, if necessary, for a slightly creamy texture.
Season with sea salt and freshly ground pepper.

3 Yukon Gold Potato Chips:
Slice the potatoes using the food slicer. Arrange the slices on the TopChips and cook in the microwave. For the ideal cooking time, refer to the instructions in The Basics.

4 To Serve:
On each Yukon gold potato chip, place ½ teaspoon caramelized onions, followed by 1 teaspoon goat cheese and one piece of fig.
Drizzle with honey.

Lamb korma on yam chips

Ingredients

For the lamb:

6 oz. lamb loin

1 tablespoon korma curry paste

1 clove garlic

1 teaspoon ground coriander

½ cup plain Greek yogurt

1 tablespoon olive oil

¼ cup mango chutney

For the chips:

4 medium-sized yams

Garnish:

2-3 sprigs fresh cilantro

1 Lamb Korma, Mango Chutney and Yogurt: Cut the lamb into ½ in. cubes. Combine the lamb, curry paste, garlic, coriander and ¼ cup Greek yogurt. Marinate overnight in the refrigerator.

2 Heat the olive oil in a sauté pan over medium-high heat. Add olive oil then add the marinated lamb.
Cook for about 4 mn until meat is slightly rose.

3 Yam Chips: Cut the yams into slices using the food slicer. Arrange them on the TopChips and cook in the microwave. For the ideal cooking time, refer to the instructions in The Basics.

4 To Serve: On each yam chip, place one cube of lamb, ½ teaspoon yogurt and ¼ teaspoon chutney.
Garnish with cilantro.

Roast duck on sweet potato chips

Ingredients

For the duck:

3-6 oz boneless duck breasts

1 tablespoon vegetable oil

sea salt, fresh ground pepper

small bunch of fresh thyme

For the black cherry compote:

2 cups water

1 cup dried tart cherries

½ vanilla bean, split lengthwise

2 pounds pitted dark cherries

2/3 cup honey

1 cinnamon stick

1 teaspoon grated lemon peel

For the chips:

2 large sweet potatoes

1 Sweet Potato Chips : Slice the sweet potatoes using the flood slicer. Place on TopChips. For the ideal cooking time, refer to the instructions in The Basics.

2 Roast duck: Preheat oven to 200°C / 375°F. Score duck breast with diamond pattern. Season duck breast on both sides with salt and pepper.

Heat a cast iron pan over medium high heat. Add oil and let heat for a few seconds. Add duck breast, skin side down. Sear for about 1 mn over medium heat. Place entire pan in preheated oven for about 12-15 mn.

Remove pan from oven. Transfer duck breasts to a sheetpan skin side up and let rest for a few minutes. When ready to serve cut duck breasts in thin slices.

3 Black cherry compote: Combine 2 cups water and dried cherries in sauce pan. Bring to boil. Reduce heat and simmer until water is reduced to ¼ cup (about 15 mn). Scrape seeds from vanilla bean and add bean. Stir in dark cherries and remaining ingredients. Simmer until cherries are tender and juice thickens (about 1 hr). Cool.
Can be made ahead.

4 To Serve: Place thin slice of duck breast on chip, garnish with a dollop of cherry compote.
Optional: garnish with thyme sprig.

Seared scallops on potato chips

Ingredients

For the peas:

1 ½ teaspoons unsalted butter

1 large shallot

1 clove garlic

½ slice pancetta

½ cup frozen peas

1/8 cup vegetable stock

1 tablespoon olive oil

Sea salt and freshly ground pepper

For the scallops:

6 scallops

1 tablespoon olive oil

For the chips:

4-5 Red Bliss potatoes

Garnish:

Salt and freshly ground pepper

12 mint leaves

1 Puréed Peas: Melt the butter in a saucepan over low heat and sauté the minced shallots and garlic. Finely chop the pancetta and add to the mixture. Cook until soft. Add the peas and vegetable stock and reduce until the liquid is gone.

Set aside to cool and use hand blender to puree until smooth. Season to taste with sea salt and freshly ground pepper.

2 Seared Scallops: Prepare the scallops by cleaning them, removing the small muscle and cutting in half horizontally. Heat a sauté pan over medium-high heat. Add olive oil and place scallops in pan, cook until lightly browned on the outside and opaque in the middle (about 1-2 mn total cooking time).

3 Red Bliss Potato Chips: Slice the Red Bliss potatoes using the food slicer. Arrange the slices on the TopChips and cook in the microwave. For the ideal cooking time, refer to the instructions in The Basics.

4 To Serve: Reheat the puréed peas and spoon ½-1 teaspoonful of the purée onto each Red Bliss potato chip (pending size of chip), followed by a seared scallop half. Season with sea salt and freshly ground pepper. Top with a mint leaf.

Tip

Add TopChips Sour Cream & Onion seasoning to your chips for extra flavor.

Tuna tartare with yukon gold potato chips

Ingredients

For the tartare:

1 teaspoon jalapeno pepper

½ tablespoon ginger

3 tablespoon grape-seed oil

1 tablespoon sweet Thai chili sauce

½ tablespoon white soy sauce

½ tablespoon rice wine vinegar

12 oz. sushi-grade Ahi tuna

For the chips:

4 medium-sized Yukon gold potatoes

Garnish:

1 avocado

1 Tuna Tartare: Seed and mince the jalapeno pepper and grate the ginger. Combine the first 6 ingredients together. Then, just before serving, toss the diced tuna in the dressing.

2 Yukon Gold Potato Chips: Slice the potatoes using the food slicer. Arrange the slices on the TopChips and cook in the microwave. For the ideal cooking time, refer to the instructions in The Basics.

3 To Serve: Spoon 1 teaspoonful of tuna tartare onto each chip and top with a piece of freshly dices avocado.

Tip
Add TopChips Salt & Vinegar seasoning to your chips for extra flavor.

Crab & mango salsa with plantain chips

Ingredients

For the salsa:

½ ripe mango

⅛ cup sweet white onion

½ teaspoon garlic

¼ teaspoon jalapeno pepper

1 ½ teaspoons fresh lime juice

1 ½ teaspoons fresh mint

1 ½ teaspoons olive oil

½ lb. fresh lump crabmeat

Sea salt and freshly ground pepper

For the chips:

2 green plantains

Garnish:

8 mint leaves

1 **Crab & Mango Salsa:** Cut the mango into ¼-in. cubes and combine in a mixing bowl with the onion, garlic, jalapeno pepper, lime juice, mint and olive oil. Refrigerate, covered, for up to 2 hrs. An hour before serving, fold in the crabmeat.

2 **Plantain Chips:** Cut the plantains in half lengthwise (about 3-4" depending size of plantain) before slicing them with the food slicer.
Arrange the slices on the TopChips and cook in the microwave. For the ideal cooking time, refer to the instructions in The Basics.

3 **To Serve:** Spoon 1 teaspoonful of the crab-and-mango salsa mixture onto each plantain chip. Garnish with julienned mint leaves.

Soup & salads

Parsnip & squash soup with pear chips

Ingredients

For the soup:

2 tablespoons olive oil

1 medium onion

2 celery stalks

2 carrots

2 shallots

1 tablespoon garlic

4 large parsnips

3 lb. delicata squash

2 pears

2 tablespoons apple cider vinegar

1.5 quarts chicken stock

Pinch cinnamon, nutmeg, cayenne pepper

For the chips:

1 pear

Garnish:

4-6 leaves of fresh sage

1 Parsnip-and- Squash Soup: In a heavy casserole, heat the olive oil over medium-high heat.

Add the chopped onion, celery, carrots and shallots. Sauté until they begin to caramelize, stirring occasionally.

Add the minced garlic and spices. Sauté for another minute.

2 Add the peeled and chopped parsnips, squash and pear.

Stir in the apple cider vinegar and chicken stock. Bring to a boil.

Reduce heat and simmer until the squash and parsnips are tender (about 30 mn).

Season to taste with sea salt and freshly ground pepper.

Remove from heat. Using hand blender, purée until smooth.

3 Pear Chips: Slice the pear halves with the food slicer. Arrange the slices on the TopChips and cook in the microwave. For the ideal cooking time, refer to the instructions in The Basics.

4 To Serve: Pour the soup into individual soup bowls and garnish with the pear chips and sage leaf.

Tip

Add TopChips Roasted Garlic seasoning to your chips for extra flavor.

Autumn beet & endive salad with apple chips

Ingredients

For the salad:

1 small red beet

1 small yellow beet

2 Belgian endives

1 large head radicchio

1 head frisée lettuce

½ cup hazelnuts

For the chips:

1 Red Delicious apple

For the vinaigrette:

2/3 cup olive oil

1 large shallot

1/3 cup apple cider vinegar

1 teaspoon Dijon mustard

1 tablespoon hazelnut oil

1 teaspoon sugar

1 Apple & carrot chips: Slice the apple and the carrot with the food slicer. Arrange them on the TopChips and cook in the microwave. For the ideal cooking time, refer to the instructions in The Basics.

2 Vinaigrette: Place the olive oil, shallot, vinegar, mustard, hazelnut oil and sugar in a blender and purée until emulsified. Season with sea salt and freshly ground pepper.

3 To Serve: Arrange the salad ingredients and apple and carrot chips on individual plates.

Drizzle with the vinaigrette just before serving.

For even more autumn flavor, you can try adding parsnip and carrot chips to this salad.

Mexican lettuce-cup salad with cotija cheese & tortilla chips

Ingredients

For the salad:

3 tablespoons olive oil

1 sweet onion

1 lb. lean ground beef

½ teaspoon Mexican oregano

Sea salt and freshly ground pepper

1 can (15 oz.) organic black beans

¼ cup chicken stock

1 head iceberg lettuce

2 diced Roma tomatoes

One 8-oz. package Cotija cheese

1 avocado

½ cup sour cream

½ cup good-quality salsa

For the chips:

8 flour tortillas

1 **Mexican Lettuce-Cup Salad with Cotija Cheese:** Heat oil in a sauté pan over medium-high heat. Add the diced onion and cook until translucent, stirring occasionally. Add the ground beef and cook until browned. Season with oregano, sea salt and freshly ground pepper.

2 Drain and rinse the black beans. Bring the black beans and chicken stock to a boil in a saucepan over medium-high heat.

3 **Flour Tortilla Chips:**
Cut the tortillas into thin strips with a knife. Arrange the strips on the TopChips and cook in the microwave. Start with 2 mn on max. power and add 15 sec increments until crisp.

4 **To Serve:**
Peel and dice the avocado. Place iceberg lettuce leaf which will act as a cup on individual plates. Add ½ cup black beans, 4 oz. ground beef, diced tomato, Cotija cheese, avocado, sour cream and salsa. Garnish with tortilla chips.

*To replace beef with chicken:
Bring 2 cups chicken broth, 1 teaspoon cumin, 1 teaspoon coriander and ½ onion, diced, to a boil. Add the chicken breasts and braise until tender (about 20-30 mn). Chop or pull apart the chicken and use instead of ground beef.

Tip

Add TopChips BBQ seasoning to your chips for extra flavor.

Cucumber-watercress salad with sumac vinaigrette & pita chips

Ingredients

For the salad:

4 Persian cucumbers

2 bunches watercress

2 large Roma tomatoes

4 oz. feta

For the vinaigrette :

4 tablespoons champagne vinegar

2 teaspoons ground sumac

1 teaspoon lemon zest

6 tablespoons extra-virgin olive oil

Sea salt and freshly ground pepper

For the chips:

2 pita bread

Ground sumac

1 Sumac vinaigrette: Combine all ingredients in a blender and emulsify.

2 Pita Chips: Cut the pita bread into small triangles with a knife. Arrange the triangles on the Mastrad TopChip and cook in the microwave. Start with 1 mn on max. power and add 15 sec increments until crisp. Season with sumac.

3 To Serve: Arrange the peeled cucumbers, stemmed watercress and quartered tomatoes on individual plates. Add the crumbled feta and pita chips and drizzle with the vinaigrette before serving.

Tip

Add TopChips Sour Cream & Onion seasoning to your chips for extra flavor.

Shrimp and watercress salad with citrus vinaigrette & mango chips

Ingredients

For the salad:

1 lb. jumbo shrimp

1 tablespoon olive oil

2 bunches watercress

1 head radicchio

2 Belgian endives

6 mint leaves

For the vinaigrette:

1 ½ teaspoons fresh grapefruit juice, fresh orange juice, fresh lemon juice

1 ½ teaspoons white balsamic vinegar

1 teaspoon grapefruit zest

1 teaspoon orange zest

1 shallot

1 tablespoon honey

1 teaspoon Dijon mustard

6 tablespoons olive oil

For the chips:

1 mango

Garnish:

2 navel oranges

4 oz package blackberries

1 Shrimp and Watercress Salad: Peel and devein the shrimp. Season them with salt and pepper.

Heat a sauté pan over high heat until almost smoking. Add the olive oil and cook the shrimp until crispy (about 1 mn); then turn them over and repeat until opaque. Remove the shrimp from the pan and set aside.

2 Citrus Vinaigrette: Place all ingredients in a blender and emulsify. Season with sea salt and freshly ground pepper.

3 Mango Chips: Slice the mango using the food slicer. Arrange the mango slices on the TopChips and cook in the microwave. For the ideal cooking time, refer to The Basics.

4 To Serve: Arrange the watercress, radicchio and endives on individual plates. Add the shrimp and mango chips and garnish with the orange segments and blackberries.

Just before serving, drizzle with the vinaigrette.

Brazilian-style barbequed pork with pickled onions & yucca chips

Ingredients

For the Pork:

One ¾-1 lb. pork tenderloin

For the barbeque sauce:

2 tablespoons vegetable oil

1 medium onion

5 cloves garlic

3 cups canned plum tomatoes

1 cup orange juice

¼ cup ketchup, red-wine vinegar, Worcestershire sauce

½ teaspoon cumin

3 tablespoons Dijon mustard

3 tablespoons brown sugar

2 tablespoons honey

¼ cup molasses

1 tablespoon achiote chili paste

3 tablespoons Mexican oregano, ancho chili powder, pasilla chili powder

2 canned chipotle chilies in adobo

For the Pickled Onions:

1 medium red onion

1 habanero chili

½ cup white vinegar

½ teaspoon Mexican oregano, sea salt

For the Chips:

1 yucca

1 Brazilian-Style Barbequed Pork: Season the pork tenderloin with sea salt and freshly ground pepper. Heat a sauté pan over medium-high heat. Add a tablespoon of olive oil and cook the pork, turning occasionally, until the meat is browned on all sides. Transfer to a 180°C / 350°F oven and roast for about 10 mn or until the meat's internal temp is 65°C / 145°F.

2 Barbeque Sauce: Heat the vegetable oil in a saucepan over medium-high heat. Add the chopped onion and cook until translucent. Add the minced garlic and cook for 1 mn. Add the remaining ingredients and bring to a boil. Reduce the heat and simmer, stirring occasionally, until thickened (about 30 mn). Using a hand blender, purée until smooth.

3 Pickled Onions: Halve and finely slice the onion. Seed and mince the chili. Combine all the ingredients. Cover and chill for at least 12 hrs.

4 Yucca Chips: Cut the yucca in slices with the food slicer. Arrange the slices on the TopChips and cook in the microwave. For the ideal cooking time, refer to the instructions in The Basics.

5 To Serve: Slice pork tenderloin on bias. Place a spoon of bbq sauce on plate, arrange half of the sliced pork tenderloin in shingled position, garnish with pickled onions, serve with yucca chips.

 ## Tip

Add TopChips BBQ seasoning to your chips for extra flavor.

Salmon on flaked vegetables

Ingredients

For the salmon:

4 salmon fillets – skin removed

1 drizzle virgin olive oil

Salt, ground pepper

For the chips:

2 average potatoes

Dried dill

1 Chips: Slice the potato chips with the food slicer and cook on TopChips. For the ideal cooking time, refer to the instructions in The Basics.
Sprinkle the chips with some dried dill before cooking.

2 Salmon: Pre-heat the oven to 180°C / 350°F. Place the salmon fillets in a steamer, drizzle some olive oil over the top and season with ground pepper. Cook for 10 mn. Take the steamer out of the oven and keep at room temperature, with the lid on, for 5 mn.

3 Presentation: Place the salmon fillets on plates, season with salt then flake the potato chips.

4 Place the dressed plates in the oven once turned off to reheat before serving.

Chicken teriyaki in fruit cases

Ingredients

For the chips:

¼ pear

¼ mango

¼ Granny Smith apple

For the chicken & its marinade:

500 g/ 1 lb organic chicken breasts

1 drizzle sesame oil

1 teaspoon fresh, chopped ginger

1 tablespoon saké

1 tablespoon Japanese vinegar

1 tablespoon honey

1 Chips: Prepare the pear, apple and mango chips with the TopChips. For the ideal cooking time, refer to the instructions in The Basics.

2 Cut the chicken breasts into small pieces, place them in a soup dish and mix into all the marinade ingredients. Cover and leave to stand at room temperature for 20 mn.

3 Drain the chicken and put the marinade to one side. Stir fry the chicken on a high heat and add the marinade once the chicken is well browned. Cook on a medium heat stirring until the sauce thickens to a syrup.

4 Crumble the fruit chips in a soup dish then roll the pieces of chicken in them. Serve straight away.

Zucchini crunchy herb crumble

Ingredients

For the chips:

½ bunch fresh flat parsley

½ bunch fresh coriander

For the crumble:

2 small courgettes/zucchinis

1 red onion

1 clove garlic

50 g/ 2 oz salted crackers

1 tablespoon chopped pecan nuts

1 drizzle olive oil

salt, ground pepper

a pinch Cayenne pepper

1 Chips: Spread the fresh herbs over the Top Chips tray, cook in the microwave on maximum power for 1 mn, leave to cool and brush off into an airtight container.

2 Pre-heat the oven to 180°C / 350°F. Prepare a pastry sheet (if you don't have one, a grill covered with greaseproof paper will do).

3 Wash the courgettes/zucchinis, chop into thin circles or slices, peel the garlic and the red onion and chop finely. Slightly brown the garlic and onion in a frying pan in a drizzle of olive oil, add the courgettes/zucchinis and brown quickly make sure to keep them crunchy. Adjust the seasoning then sprinkle with Cayenne pepper.

4 Place the pastry circle on the baking sheet. Fill them with the courgettes/zucchinis and pat down gently.

5 Mix the crushed crackers and the chopped pecan nuts in a bowl. Add two tablespoons of dried herbs and cover the courgettes/zuchinis with this mixture. Place in the oven on 180°C / 350°F for 5 mn then place under a grill until the crumble browns slightly.

6 Place the circles on your plates and turn out when ready to serve.

Tip

Add TopChips Sour Cream & Onion seasoning to your chips for extra flavor.

entrées

Steamed cod with heirloom tomatoes, sautéed spinach & yukon gold potato chips

Ingredients

For the cod:

1 lemon

2, 6 oz. portions of fresh cod

2 tablespoons olive oil

6 oz. baby heirloom tomatoes

2 sprigs fresh marjoram

1 teaspoon fresh lemon juice

For the spinach:

1 tablespoon olive oil

1 large shallot

6 oz. fresh Bloomsdale spinach

Sea salt and freshly ground pepper

For the chips:

2 Yukon gold potatoes, washed

Sea salt and freshly ground pepper

1 Steamed Cod with Heirloom Tomatoes:
In a steam cooker, place: half the thinly sliced lemon, one 6-oz. portion of cod, drizzled with olive oil, half the tomatoes, 1 sprig marjoram and half the lemon juice. Cook in the microwave for 4 mn (the cod should be opaque and flakey).

2 Sautéed Spinach: Heat oil in a sauté pan over medium-high heat. Add the minced shallot and cook until slightly translucent (about 1-2 mn). Then add the spinach and season with sea salt and freshly ground pepper.
Sauté just until wilted.
Transfer to a wire rack over a baking sheet to drain.

3 Yukon Gold Potato Chips:
Slice the potatoes using the food slicer. Arrange the slices on the TopChips and cook in the microwave. For the ideal cooking time, refer to the instructions in The Basics. Season with sea salt and freshly ground pepper.

4 To Serve: Arrange potato chips on plate, place half of the sautéed spinach on each plate. Place portion of cod on spinach. Pour tomato-natural jus marjoram mixture over the cod.

Tip
Add TopChips Roasted Garlic seasoning to your chips for extra flavor.

Braised beef short ribs with parsnip chips

Ingredients

For the ribs:

6 14-oz. beef short ribs, bone-in

Sea salt and freshly ground pepper

½ cup extra-virgin olive oil

1 cup sweet onion

½ cup carrot

½ cup celery

1 package frozen pearl onions

1 small bunch fresh thyme sprigs

2 fresh bay leaves

2 tablespoons balsamic vinegar

2 cups port

2 cups red wine

6 cups beef stock

1 small bunch flat-leaf parsley

For the chips:

4 large parsnips

1 Braised Beef Short Ribs: A day ahead, season the short ribs with sea salt and freshly ground pepper. Cover and refrigerate overnight.
The next day, preheat the oven to 190°C / 375°F.

2 Heat the olive oil in a cast iron casserole (large enough to hold the ribs in a single layer). When almost smoking, add the short ribs and sear until browned on all sides. Remove the ribs and set aside.

3 In the same pan, reduce the heat to medium and add the diced onion, carrot and celery. Add the frozen pearl onions. Scrap the bottom of the pan regularly; cook until the vegetables are caramelized. Add the balsamic vinegar, port and red wine. Pour in the beef stock and increase the heat to high. Boil the liquid until reduced by one-third.

4 Add short ribs to the casserole , add the parsley and cover. Braise on top of stove over medium-low heat or in oven at 175°C / 350°F for about 3 hours.

5 Parsnip Chips: Slice the parsnips with the mandolin. Arrange the slices on the TopChips and cook in the microwave. For the ideal cooking time, refer to the instructions in The Basics.

6 To Serve: With a slotted spoon, arrange a bed of vegetables on individual plates, followed by a braised short rib. Garnish with the parsnip chips.

Rice pudding, pear compote, pear chip garnish

Ingredients

For the rice pudding:

5 cups whole milk

1 cup Arborio rice

½ cup sugar

1 vanilla bean

1 tsp cinnamon
or 2 cinnamon sticks

For the compote:

4 medium pears

½ cup brown sugar

2 tablespoon cream

1 Pear Chips: Cut pear in half, slice on food slicer. Place chips on TopChips and cooking microwave according to directions found in The Basics.

2 Heat the milk, sugar, vanilla bean, cinnamon over medium high heat. Bring to boil, add rice and reduce heat to simmer, stirring occasionally, for about 25-30 mn or until rice is tender and creamy.

3 Melt butter in sauté pan over medium high heat. Add pears and cook, stirring occasionally for about 4-5 mn or until tender and golden brown. Add sugar and cream, cook some more stirring occasionally, for 3 more minutes until sauce thickens slightly.

4 Place in serving bowls, add teaspoon of compote and a pear chip to serve.

difficulty
★ ★ ★

preparation
20 mn
cooking
1 hr

Serves
8

Lime cheese-cake with crispy mango

Ingredients

For the cake:

200 g/ 7 oz biscuits

125 g/ 4 ½ oz melted butter

500 g/ 1 lb philadelphia cheese

150 g/ 5 oz caster sugar

2 tablespoons flour

3 eggs

250 ml/ 8 ½ fl oz fresh cream

1 tablespoon lime zest

1 Chips: Prepare the mango chips with the Top Chips as indicated in the instructions in The Basics.

2 Crush the biscuits and mix in with the crumbled mango chips. Add the butter and mix to form a paste. Cover the bottom of the cake pan with this mixture then put the cake pan in the fridge for 1 hour.

3 Pre-heat the oven to 180°C / 350°F.

4 Whisk the egg whites, add the sugar and flour then the yolks one by one. Add the cream and the lime zest.

5 Pour the mixture over the biscuit base in the cake pan and place in the oven for 50 mn until the cake is firm to the touch.

6 Leave to cool, gently turn out and serve cold. Decorate with the mango chips.

Quince-apple crumble with vanilla ice cream and apple chips

Ingredients

For the topping:

1 cup all-purpose flour

½ cup brown sugar & rolled oats

1 stick chilled unsalted butter

½ cup chopped walnuts

For the filling:

2 quinces

3 Granny Smith apples

1 teaspoon lemon juice

½ cup sugar

¼ cup brown sugar

1 tablespoon flour

½ teaspoon rosemary

For the chips:

1 Granny Smith apple

Garnish:

4 scoops vanilla ice cream

1 Crumble Topping: Combine the flour, brown sugar and oats in a mixing bowl. Use your fingertips or pastry cutter to work in the butter pieces until large clumps form. Add the chopped walnuts.

2 Quince-Apple Filling: Toss the peeled and cubed quinces and apples in the lemon juice. Toss with brown and granulated sugar. Add the flour and rosemary. Divide mixture among 4 ramekins or small oven proof dishes. Cover with the crumble topping and bake at 180°C / 350°F until the quince-apple mixture is bubbling and the topping is golden-brown (about 40-45 mn).

3 Apple chips: Slice the apple with the food slicer. Arrange them on the TopChips and cook in the microwave. For the ideal cooking time, refer to the instructions in The Basics.

4 To Serve: Top each serving of crumble with a scoop of vanilla ice cream and an apple chip.

Tip

Add TopChips apple pie seasoning to your chips for extra flavor.

Mini crispy carrot cake

Ingredients

For the chips:

1 carrot

1 pinch cumin

For the cakes:

2 eggs

100 g/ 4 oz flour

50 g/ 2 oz unsalted butter

50 g/ 2 oz sugar

1 good sized carrot

½ tablespoon baking powder

1 Chips: Prepare the chips with the TopChips as indicated in the instructions in The Basics.

2 Cakes: Pre-heat the oven to 180°C / 350°F.

3 Mix the eggs and sugar in a round bottomed bowl. Whisk until whitened. Melt the butter and add it to the mixture. Pour the flour and baking powder in, from a height, mix gently. Finely grate the carrot and add it to the mixture.

4 Share the mixture between the 8 moulds.
Crush the carrot chips and sprinkle over the cakes.
Cook for 15 mn.
Leave to cool before turning out.
Eat whilst warm.

Apples galore!

Ingredients

For the chips:

2 Granny Smith apples

For the preparation:

4 Granny Smith apples

3 ripe Golden delicious apples

3 sheets gelatine

50 g/ 2 oz caster sugar

1 tablespoon soft brown sugar

1 vanilla pod

1 lime

1 Chips: Make two Granny Smith apples into chips, with the TopChips as indicated in the instructions in The Basics.

2 Mouse: Wash the Golden Delicious apples then put them in a blender or juice extractor to collect the juice.
Pass through a fine sieve and gently heat in a pan with 2 oz of caster sugar.
Soften the gelatine in a bowl of cold water and whisk into the hot apple, once off the heat.
Pour the apple juice mixture into the base of the cream whipper, insert a gas cartridge and lay on its side in the fridge for at least 2 hours.

3 Uncooked compote: Grate the 2 remaining Granny Smith apples. Place them in a bowl and sprinkle with soft brown sugar. Add the lime zest and vanilla seeds. Cover and place in the fridge until ready to serve.

4 Presentation: Place the grated apples in a glass dessert bowl, vigorously shake the cream whipper and place some of the emulsion on top. Top with some dried apple chips. Eat straight away.

 ## Tip

Add TopChips Apple Pie seasoning to your chips for extra flavor.

Cranberry oatmeal with granola & apple chips

Ingredients

For the oatmeal:

4 cups water

½ teaspoon sea salt

2 cups organic rolled oats

1 cup milk

2 tablespoons brown sugar

2 tablespoon unsalted organic butter

4 tablespoons organic granola

1 cup dried cranberries

Organic maple syrup

For the chips:

1 Granny Smith apple

1 Cranberry Oatmeal with Granola: Bring the water and ½ teaspoon sea salt to a boil in large saucepan. Add the organic rolled oats and reduce the heat. Cook 10-15 mn.

Stir in the milk, brown sugar and butter; let stand for a few minutes. Stir in the granola and dried cranberries.

2 Apple chips: Slice the apple with the food slicer. Arrange them on the TopChips and cook in the microwave. For the ideal cooking time, refer to the instructions in The Basics.

3 To Serve: Divide the oatmeal mixture among 4 bowls and add extra granola, dried cranberries, brown sugar and a pat of butter on top. Drizzle with maple syrup and garnish with apple chips.

Recipes: Credits

Jean-Claude Fascina, Consultant Chef: p.24, 26, 30, 60, 62, 64, 74, 78, 80
Camille Renk, Consultant Chef: p. 18, 20, 22, 30, 32, 34, 36, 38, 40, 42, 46, 48, 50, 52, 54, 58, 66, 68, 72, 76, 82

Photos: Credits
Julien Bouvier: p. 14, 16 to 82
Studio 1+1: cover & p. 6, 8 to 13

Special thanks to **Sabine Bernert**, collection editor of the original edition.

© 2012 Mastrad
Les Indispensables de Mastrad – Chips
Registration of Copyright
Printing completed by Xinlian
Artistic Printing Cie / China

Mastrad SA
32 bis-34, bd de Picpus
75012 Paris
FRANCE
Tél : +33 (1) 49 26 96 00
Fax : +33 (1) 49 26 96 06
www.mastrad.fr